A GLANCE AT POETRY

FROM MY DESK TO YOURS

CHETANYA SWAMI

To God, who gives me strength and inspiration,

I dedicate this book with deep appreciation.

To my teachers, who have guided me with their wisdom,

I thank you for your guidance and freedom

To allow me to explore, to learn, and to grow.

You have helped me to blossom and to show

The world the beauty that lies within.

For this, I am forever grateful and will always grin.

To my family, who have always been my rock,

I thank you for your love, support, and never-ending shock

At the things I do and the paths I choose.

You have been there for me, no matter what the news.

And to my friends, who have stood by my side,

I thank you for your friendship, laughter, and pride

In all that I have accomplished.

You have helped me to shine.

I am grateful for your presence in my life, all the time.

Finally, to my readers, who have picked up this book,

I thank you for your time and for taking a look

At the words I have written.

May they touch your heart,

And may this dedication, from the very start,

Set the tone for the journey we are about to embark.

Contents

Contents

Contents

Foreword

Dear readers,

A story unfolds within these pages,

A tale of hard work, dedication, and creative rages.

Chetanya's passion for the written word,

Is captured here, in this book, to be heard.

Through words and phrases, she paints a scene,

Sharing with us her hopes and her keen

Her thoughts and ideas, so clearly conveyed,

Will leave you thinking, and wanting more, unafraid.

It is my great pleasure to introduce,

This masterpiece, created by one of our muse.

Let us all take the time to read,

And appreciate dear Chetanya as she continues to seed.

So let us celebrate, this achievement grand,

Congratulations to our dear child , for taking a stand.

Sincerely,

Reena Chakravorty

Principal

Preface

Dear reader,

Welcome to this collection of poetry. Within these pages, you will find a diverse array of themes and styles, all united by the common thread of the written word. Poetry has the unique ability to distill complex emotions and ideas into concise, powerful language, and I hope that these poems will resonate with you on a deep level.

As you journey through this book, allow yourself to be transported to new worlds, to feel a wide range of emotions, and to see the world in a different light. Whether you are an experienced poetry enthusiast or a newcomer to the form, I hope that you will find something in these pages that speaks to you.

I have always found solace in the written word and have turned to poetry as a means of self-expression and understanding. I hope that these poems will speak to you in some way and provide a glimpse into my world.

I thank you for taking the time to read these poems and for allowing me to share a part of myself with you. I hope that you find something here that resonates with you and stays with you long after you have finished reading.

Thank you for joining me on this literary journey.

Sincerely,

Chetanya Swami (Chets)

Acknowledgements

"To God, who has blessed me with the talent and drive to write poems and share them with others. Your guidance and inspiration have been invaluable to me.

To my teachers, who have imparted their knowledge and wisdom upon me and helped to shape me into the person and writer I am today. Your influence has been instrumental in my journey as an writer

To my family, who have always supported and encouraged my love of storytelling. Thank you for believing in me and for being my biggest fans.

To my friends, who have listened to my ideas, provided invaluable feedback and encouragement, and been a constant source of support and motivation. Your encouragement and camaraderie have meant the world to me.

To my readers, thank you for taking the time to delve into the world I have created. It is my hope that you will find something within these pages that resonates with you and stays with you long after you've finished reading.

This book is dedicated to all of you, with love and gratitude."

Prologue

Ink on the page,

A story to engage,

A journey for the mind,

To leave behind the grind.

Words flowing like a stream,

Emotions running wild,

The rhythm and the rhyme,

A beauty to behold.

So come and take a stroll,

With me down this road,

Where verse and poetry,

Forever will unfold.

A world of endless possibility,

Brought to life with every pen stroke,

A tapestry of melodies,

Enwrapped within each verse spoke.

The magic of the written word,

A treasure to be found,

In each and every poem,

A beauty so profound.

So let us lose ourselves,

In this poetic realm,

Where magic and wonder,

Forever do overwhelm.

1. Poetry

To compliment my first poetry book heres a work on Poetry
Poetry, oh poetry
A language all its own
With words that twist and dance
In rhythms free to roam
It speaks to the soul
In ways that mere prose cannot
It touches the heart
In a way that others cannot
It's a fire that burns
A passion that ignites
A way to express
All the love, pain, and light
So let the poetry flow
From pen to paper, heart to soul
For in its lines and stanzas
Poetry, a source of wonder
We find a place to be whole
A way to capture truth
It speaks to the ages
And holds a timeless youth
It defies conventions
And breaks all the rules
It's a form of expression
That's both intimate and cool

It paints pictures with words
And tells stories that sing
It's a way to share emotions
In a way that is both raw and refined
So let the poetry flow
Like a river of gold
For in its verse and rhyme
We find a place to unfold
It's a treasure to be savored
A gift to be embraced
For in the world of poetry
We find a place to be grace

2. Lost in a book

The feeling of getting lost in a book
Is like falling into a dream
Where the pages take you away
To a place you've never been before
And you can stay there forever
If you want to
There's nothing quite like it
The feeling of getting lost in a book
Forgetting the world around you
And losing yourself in another
It's a feeling like no other
And one that I can't get enough of
When I'm lost in a book
I feel like I can do anything
And go anywhere
I'm free to be whoever I want to be
And there's no limit to what I can do
It's a feeling I can't describe
But one that I absolutely love
And one that I hope to feel again and again

3. Books

Books are my favorite things
I can spend hours upon hours
Just sitting and reading
I can travel to different places
And meet new people
All without leaving my chair
I can be anyone I want to be
And do anything I can imagine
When I open up a book
There are no limits
To what I can do
And I can't wait to see
What new adventures await me
In the pages of a book

4. In the still of the night

In the still of the night,
when the world is at rest,
I find solace in the moonlight,
and peace in its gentle caress.
The stars twinkle above,
like diamonds in the sky,
and I am filled with love,
for the world and all that lies within.
In this moment of calm,
I am at one with all,
the past and future, the present and all,
In this place, I stand tall.
So let the winds of change blow,
and the thunder roll,
for I am at peace,
in this still and silent whole.

5. Nature

The sky so blue, the grass so green
The trees so tall, the flowers so serene
The river flows, the mountains rise
Nature's beauty never fails to surprise
The sun so bright, the moon so fair
The stars so twinkly, the air so rare
The birds they sing, the bees they hum
Nature's beauty is never done
The ocean waves, the sandy shore
The dolphins play, the whales do more
The coral reefs, the fish so fine
Nature's beauty is truly divine
So let us take a moment to appreciate
The wonders of the natural state
For without it, our lives would be incomplete
Nature's beauty is a gift, so sweet

6. War and Peace

War and peace, two sides of a coin
One brings destruction, the other joy
War rages on, with battles to be fought
Leaving behind a trail of blood and destruction
Peace, on the other hand, is a gentle breeze
Blowing through fields of green and gold
Bringing with it hope and happiness
A chance for a new beginning, a chance to be whole
But these two forces are always at odds
One trying to conquer and destroy
The other trying to heal and rebuild
Leaving us to wonder which one will win
Oh, war and peace, a never-ending cycle
Of destruction and rebuilding, of hate and love
But perhaps one day we'll find a way
To bring about an end to this cycle
And live in a world where war and peace coexist
Where everyone is free to live and love
In a world of harmony, a world of bliss
That's the world we all dream of

7. Languages

Languages, a tapestry of words
A patchwork of sounds, a multitude of verbs
Each one unique, each one distinct
A way to express, to connect
From ancient tongues to modern speech
Languages bring people within reach
Of one another, across lands and seas
Bridging gaps, bringing unity
Languages, a tool for communication
A way to share thoughts, ideas, and imagination
A way to connect with history and culture
Languages, a beautiful feature
So let us embrace the diversity
Of languages, and all they bring to society
A wealth of expression, a joy to hear
Languages, a treasure beyond measure.

8. Bharatanatyam

Bharatanatyam, dance divine
Rooted in tradition, yet forever fine
Graceful and fluid, every movement precise
A true art form, a cultural treasure to suffice
With rhythmic feet and graceful hand
This dance tells stories of a distant land
Elegant poses and intricate steps
A feast for the eyes, a true masterpiece
The music fills the air, the beats vibrate
As the dancer moves with utmost grace
A beautiful expression of culture and art
Bharatanatyam, a true work of heart
So let us all take a moment to appreciate
This beautiful dance, a true cultural gem
Bharatanatyam, a treasure to behold
Forever etched in the stories of old
Bharatanatyam, a dance of pure delight
It fills the soul and takes flight
From the ancient temples to the modern stage
This dance remains, a true masterpiece of age
With every step, a tale is told
Of love and loss, of joy and old
The dancer moves with grace and poise
A true artist, with talent and voice
The costumes bright and colors bold

Add to the beauty, to behold
The music fills the air, the beats resound
As the dancer takes her place on the ground
So let us all take a moment to appreciate
This beautiful dance, a true cultural fate
Bharatanatyam, a treasure to behold
Forever etched in the stories of old

9. The Sun Is Shining Bright

The sun is shining bright
The birds are singing sweet
The world is a beautiful sight
Our feet can't be beat
We stand tall and proud
Our hearts are full of cheer
We shout out loud
There's nothing to fear
We face each day with grace
And embrace the unknown
We find our own pace
And make our own home
We chase our dreams
And never look back
We know it seems
We're on the right track
So let's keep on going
And never lose sight
Of all the things we're knowing
And all the love in sight
For life is a journey
And it's ours to explore
So let's make it merry
And never be a bore
For the world is ours to take

And we have the power within
So let's not make any mistakes
And let our light always beam

10. Mirror Self

A mirror self, a reflection true
A counterpart, a copy of you
A twin, a shadow, a doppelganger
A being that's familiar, yet stranger
You stare into the glass, and what do you see?
Is it you, or a version of you that's incomplete?
The mirror self stares back, with eyes just like yours
But do they see the same things, or have different allures?
Sometimes the mirror self seems wiser than you
A voice of reason, when all you can do is stew
Other times it's a trickster, a deceiver, a cheat
Leading you astray, and making your life incomplete
But whether friend or foe, the mirror self remains
A constant presence, through joy and through pains
It's a part of you, like it or not
So embrace it, and all the things that it's got
For the mirror self is more than just a surface reflection
It's a symbol of self, and all its imperfections
So look into the glass, and see who you are
Embrace your mirror self, and shine like a star

11. Mathematics : Infinity

The concept of infinity
Is a strange and curious thing
It's a number that goes on forever
And it can make your head spin and sing
It's not something you can count to
Or put in a box or a bag
It's a number without an end
That can make you feel both small and sad
But infinity is also beautiful
In the way it defies all bounds
It's a number that's infinite
And that makes it truly profound
So let's embrace the mystery
Of this infinite number we see
For it's a concept that's truly great
And it's a joy for you and me

12. From The Desk Of A Ghost

I am a ghost, a spirit adrift
Trapped in this world, unable to lift
The veil that separates me from the living
Forever watching, forever unforgiving
I walk among you, unseen and unheard
A forgotten soul, my words left blurred
But I am here, a presence unseen
Trapped in this world, my life a dream
I long to be free, to break these chains
To rise above, to shed these pains
But until then, I am doomed to roam
A ghost among you, forever alone.

13. Ghostwriter

Imagine an invisible ghost
Picking up a pen with a ghostly hand
And starting to write to you
On a page that you can't see
It's a strange and eerie feeling
To know that someone unseen
Is communicating with you
In a way that's truly unique
But as the words start to form
And the poem begins to take shape
You can't help but feel a sense of wonder
At the power of the written word
So let the ghost continue to write
Let the words flow onto the page
For even though the hand may be ghostly
The message is still very real.

14. "Have a good day, now"

"Have a good day, now"
The words, so simple and true
Spoken with a smile and a nod
To a stranger, just passing through
We shared a moment, brief and fleet
But still, it filled my heart with cheer
A simple greeting, kind and sweet
To start my day, so bright and clear
We went our separate ways, it's true
But still, that moment lingers on
A stranger's kindness, pure and true
A memory, now forever drawn
I think of that encounter now
And how it left me feeling light
A momentary connection, somehow
A small but precious spark of light
So here's to strangers, kind and true
Who brighten up our days with ease
May we all be reminded anew
To pay it forward, and to never cease
To spread a little joy and cheer
To those we meet along the way
For a kind word can mean so much
And brighten up someone's day

15. Life is a journey

Life is a journey, filled with ups and downs,

But no matter what, don't let your spirit drown.

When times are tough, and you feel all alone,

Just remember, you are stronger than you've ever known.

You have the power to overcome any fear,

Just close your eyes, and visualize your future clear.

You have the determination, the drive, and the heart,

So don't let anyone tell you, you'll never play a part.

In this world, filled with endless possibilities,

You have the potential, to achieve your wildest dreams.

So don't give up, no matter how hard it may seem,

You have the courage, to chase your dreams and gleam.

16. The Darkness of The Night

The darkness of the night
Brings tears to my eyes
As I think of all the things
That I have left behind
The loneliness and sadness
That fills my soul
Seems to have no end
As I wander through this cold
The memories of love and joy
That once filled my heart
Now seem so far away
As I tear myself apart
I try to find the light
But it seems so hard to see
In this endless cycle
Of melancholy
But even in these darkest hours
I hold on to hope and faith
That one day the sun will shine
And banish all this hate.

17. Is Someone There?

I need a caring shoulder
But I am the only one here
I want someone to listen
But I am an only ear
Dealing with despair
Nobody's there to care
Can someone be there
It's dark and lonely here
Voices in my mind
Forcing from behind
Telling I should die
There's no reason why
Does anybody love me?
Would they shed a tear?
Would anybody even care
If I were to disappear?
My nature is bad
but not by choice.
How would you feel
with an unheard voice?
My smile hides my tears.
My laugh hides my screams.
It's been this way for years.
Things aren't as they seem.
The darkness surrounds me.

It's getting so cold.
I'm all alone
With no one to hold.

It's getting so cold.
I'm all alone
With no one to hold.

18. Misfit

Trapped inside my personal hell,
Where nobody hears my yell
There's something that mutes my pain
All my efforts are going vain
Voices in my head are unbearable
All they say is that I am terrible
I feel that I don't fit in
There's something wrong with my skin
Wish someone out there had something to say
Even as simple as a hey!
They make me so much better
With just a mixture of these three letter
Would love to have someone's concern
Before I burn
Oh! How blue I am
To learn to smile I'll have to cram

19. Depression

Depression is a monster
That destroys both heart and soul
It tortures without mercy
And consumes it's victim whole
The monster is my friend, it lays under my bed
It counts the tears that I shed
Doesn't go away
Promised that it will stay
Some people are sad
From the time that they are young
Sadness is considered bad
To control my tears, my head swung
Everyone has a sea
They are drowning in
Feel they've been stung by a bee
And have committed a sin
Parents drowning in their own
They say that you have grown
They forget to take care
Another reason for despair
We don't want sympathy
Just want you to be aware
That you can nurture others
And help by taking care

20. Behind My Smile

Behind my smile is a heart that's broken
A soul that's weary, a spirit that's choked
By the weight of the world, and the words left unspoken
By the pain of the past, and the fear of the future
But despite it all, I wear a smile on my face
For it's the only armor I have to defend
Against the doubts and the fears that chase
And the loneliness that seems to never end
So I paste on a grin, and I hold my head high
And I laugh and I joke, and I do my best to shine
For I know that one day, this darkness will pass by
And the sun will rise again, and I'll be just fine
Until then, I'll keep smiling, through the joy and the pain
For it's the only way I know how to survive
In this crazy, mixed-up world, where nothing is certain
But the love that I have, and the hope that I carry
Inside my heart, behind my smile.

21. Mirrors Also Lie

Mirrors also lie,
For they only show what's on the outside,
They hide the truth that lies within,
The beauty that is held within.
They reflect the surface,
But cannot capture the depth,
The soul that shines within,
The love that knows no end.
So don't believe all that you see,
For mirrors also lie,
They show but a fraction,
Of the person standing by.

22. Dream!

Dream Dream Dream
There's no need to hear your minds useless scream
You might feel like you are not good enough
And the competition is really tough
But trust me you are a star
Born to shine
Your destination may seem far
Still your experiments will come out fine
Remember try,try
But never cry
And you're halfway there
Then your success is something that you wil share

Think that you are the best
And life's an easy test
You"ll pass with flying colors
Don't make your life duller

23. The Silent Screaming Voices

The voices in my head
Want me to go to bed
Cannot hear a single voice say
Wakeup! Shine! It's a new day
My mind goes blank
As I see someone online do a plank
Insecurities creep in
Wish I could throw them in the bin
The work is due tomorrow
I should rather be in sorrow
People say that life's a test
Who ll help me get out of this quest
This hectic life tires me
What if my boss fires me
Let's take a moment out of this mess
We will be out of this I guess
Wish I could fly high
Beyond the sky
Outwith the clouds
Where genuine people ask my whereabouts

24. Life

Sadly,life isn't fair
But don't be in despair
Forget the harsh realities
And dive into some fantasies
I know you have had sleepless nights
Trying to fight with your mights
Don't worry we have all been there
There's a lot we had to bare
Believing we aren't good enough
As we had to hear things that are gruff
We need to learn not to lose hope
To survive you should learn to cope

25. Young Person, Old Soul

A young soul in an old mind,

Though youth surrounds, it's wisdom you'll find.

Eyes that have seen more than years can tell,

A heart that's lived through life's highs and hells.

You walk with grace, with a steady pace,

And in your words, there's a certain grace.

You listen well, and you speak with care,

For the weight of the world, you seem to bear.

You've known love, and you've known loss,

You've felt the pain, and the cost.

But through it all, you've risen above,

For your spirit is strong, and your heart is love.

Though you may be young, your soul is old,

And in this world, your story's been told.

So keep on living, and keep on growing,

For the world needs more souls like yours, glowing.

26. Perfection

Perfection, a thing so fine
A goal we all strive to find
But in our quest, we often stray
From the present moment, and lose our way
We strive for perfection in all we do
But in this pursuit, we often miss the view
The beauty in the mess, the art in the flaw
The love in the imperfect, the good in the raw
For perfection is an illusion, a mirage in the sand
A constant chase, a never-ending demand
But true contentment comes from within
When we let go of perfection, and embrace our kin
So let go of the crave, and find peace within
Embrace the imperfect, and let perfection begin

27. Daydreams vs Reality

In my daydreams, I am free
To fly to distant lands and see
The wonders of the world unfold
In a tapestry of stories told
But reality is a different tune
A constant hum that never ends
It anchors me to solid ground
As my feet firmly plant
But still, I find myself drifting
To a place where the grass is greener
Where anything is possible
And my wildest dreams come true
For in the realm of daydreams
I am limitless and brave
But in reality, I am human
And my limits I must face
Yet I will always keep on dreaming
For it's the only way to keep alive
The hope that one day, reality
Will match the magic I contrive

28. Rat Race

A rat race it is, my friend,
A never-ending, endless blend
Of hustle and bustle, day and night
A constant struggle, a never-ending fight
We work and work, with little rest
Trying to keep up, do our best
We run and run, trying to keep pace
But somehow, we never seem to win this race
We chase and chase, our tails in view
Trying to outdo, to come out on top
But in the end, what do we gain?
A pile of riches, a life of pain?
So let us pause, take a step back
And think about what it is we lack
Perhaps it's time to slow down, to rest
And find a way to truly be blessed.

29. Rainbow After The Storm

Hues of red and orange,

Blend together like a dream, A fire in the night sky, A glowing, vibrant gleam.

Soft shades of yellow, Brighter than the morning sun, A warming presence, A beautiful one.

Green, the color of life, Fresh and new, A calming presence, A sight to view.

Blue, the color of the sea, Mysterious and deep, A cool and tranquil feeling, An endless, soothing sleep.

Purple, a regal hue, Rich and grand, A symbol of power, A sight to stand.

All these colors swirling, In a beautiful array, A wondrous display, Of beauty every day.

30. Colours

A splash of vibrant energy,

A burst of pure delight,

A swirl of rich, bold passion,

A sight to ignite.

A wash of gentle soothing,

A calm and peaceful hue,

A touch of gentle grace,

A sight to renew.

A shimmer of sparkling magic,

A hint of pure delight,

A burst of playful joy,

A sight to ignite.

A swirl of deep, intense mystery,

A rich, dark shade of night,

A hint of hidden secrets,

A sight to ignite.

A burst of bright, shining sunshine,

A warm and radiant glow,

A symbol of hope and happiness,

A sight to behold.

All these colors swirling,

In a beautiful array,

A wondrous display,

Of beauty every day.

31. Indian Cuisine

Indian cuisine, so rich and so diverse

From north to south, east to west, it does traverse

From the spicy curries of the west

To the tangy pickles of the east

There's the tandoori chicken of the north

And the seafood of the south

There's the biryani, oh so grand

And the naan, soft and never bland

The flavors, oh so bold and bright

The aromas, a treat for the sight

The diversity, a true delight

Indian cuisine, a culinary delight

There's the chaat, a street food delight

And the samosas, a crispy fried delight

There's the pakoras, so tasty and light

And the kebabs, a BBQ delight

The desserts, oh so sweet and divine

The gulab jamun, a syrup soaked delight

The kulfi, a creamy frozen treat

And the ras malai, a cheese ball so neat

Indian cuisine, a culinary wonder

A true reflection of the land and its culture

So diverse, yet so united Indian cuisine, a true pride

32. Who am I?

Some say that I am kind
And my personality isn't refined
They say that I am amazing
But I hate when they are appraising
They tell me to be myself
But hate when I be
What they want on my soul's shelf
I can never see
People see me as a talkative person
And they really like my assertion
I feel that I am the best
And life's taking a test.
But nobody asked do I really want to talk?
Or I just need a quiet walk
They make do what they want
And I agree as I won't like if they daunt
Wait does that mean I am a people pleaser
And I am not a teaser
Is that good?
Or just a thing everyone does in childhood?
The answer for who I am?
I'll have to cram
People describe me is various ways
I don't know what the right one says
Can someone teach me how to define myself?

That would be a great help

I make sure I don't break a delph

So that I won't have to welp

I have no idea about myself

I keep adding books to my bookshelf

Am I an avid reader then?

Who I am I'll learn one day but I don't know when.

33. Cancerians

According to my zodiac, I am a cancerian. So heres a poem dedicated
to all my fellow cancerians.

Cancerians, oh Cancerians,

So sensitive and kind,

Your hearts are filled with love and care,

For others, all the time.

Your emotional depths run deep,

You wear your heart on your sleeve,

Your intuition guides you well

You always seem to achieve.

You're nurturing and protective,

Of those you hold dear,

You'll go to great lengths,

To keep those you love, near.

Cancerians, oh Cancerians,

You have a strength within,

That sees you through the toughest times,

And helps you to begin again.

So here's to you, dear Cancerians,

May your lives be blessed,

May your hearts be filled with joy,

And all your worries be put to rest.

Cancerians, oh Cancerians,

Your home is your haven,

You love to create a cozy space,

Where you can relax and unwind.

Your moods may wax and wane,

Like the phases of the moon,

But your loved ones know,

That your love will come through.

You're fiercely loyal,

And fiercely independent too,

You march to the beat of your own drum,

And that's something to be true.

So here's to you, dear Cancerians,

May your world be filled with love,

May you always find the comfort,

In the ones you hold above.

And when the going gets tough,

And the road gets rough,

Just remember, Cancerians,

You're strong enough.

34. To My Younger Self

My younger self
I hope you have filled your shelf
I hope you are not blue
I don't say it but I love you!
Oh How much you suffered
Happy memories you couldn't afford
How much you cried
I know to stop sobbing you tried
Let me tell you a secret
The world is a mess
That doesn't mean you need to take stress
They ask you how you have been
You suffering they have barely seen
The truth is that everything in life
Can be perfectly fine
If you learn to strife
And with your favorite people you dine
Now look and me
How much I have changed
I shout in glee
My happiness I have arranged
I am your older self
I write to you
Keep arranging your bookshelf
Once again I love you

• 41 •

35. Solitude

Do we cry to heal ourselves?
Or do we cry to seal ourselves?
Laugh and the world laughs with you
Weep and you weep alone
That's what we have learnt
What to do if our heart is burnt?
Everything's on fire
You cannot fulfill your desire
You shed tears
No one hears
You are left all alone
So that you can moan
So when we let out a raking sob,
With a hand cupped so closely to our cheek,
Is our desire to be heard,
Or to just let the pain slowly leak?

36. Pariksha Pe Charcha

When the session ends
A student wends
Shows a lot of determination
To prepare for one's examination
We all feel stressed
And everything seems messed
There's no time to waste
As we are being raced
Then just before our exam
'Pariksha Pe Charcha', by our Prime Minister came to rescue
Taught us there's no need to cram
Just find what works best for you
We learnt that technology is a boon not a curse
It's in our hands if we make it worse
Celebrate an exam like a festival
And try not to hustle
Competition is the best part of life
That's how we learn to thrive
Working on ourselves continuously
And taking decisions cautiously
Marks do not matter
But that doesn't mean we should smatter
Just try to give your best
Because it's just a test

37. For My Teachers

I'm happy that you're my teacher;
I enjoy each lesson you teach.
As my role model you inspire me
To dream and to work and to reach.
For reaching deep in me
to find all I can be
before I can see it myself.
You never gave up on me.
I have a future
because of you.
I always love your class;
Your teaching helps me see,
That to have a happy life,
Positivity is the key.

38. Dark Days

There will be dark days,
when you feel alone
with your aching heart
but that doesn't mean
you will always be.
The days shall pass
Just build up strength
Just like passing a class
Be on the same wavelength
I know the stormy nights
Where the raindrops are your tears
Fighting with your mights
Hoping that someone cares
I am here to tell
There is no need to worry
I will cast a sweet spell
Just don't be in a hurry

39. Crave for Perfection

Perfection oh! What is it?
For me it's always a skit
Where I pretend to be my best
When life's taking a test
I feel like a butterfly
Just wanting to cry
Who pays any attention?
No one I can mention
Always wanting to be perfect
It's untouchable
Have I been wrecked?
It always feels dull
I was searching for something,
but I didn't know where to look.
I searched for so long,
and all my time it took.
What was I looking for,
or what was looking for me?
My eyes I kept open,
but I just couldn't see.

40. Friends

From the day that I first knew you,
Your heart was pure and kind;
Your smile was sweet and innocent,
Your wit was well refined.
You gave me strength to carry on
Even when all hope
Seemed to be gone
You taught me how to cope
Happiness turned into scrappiness
I lean on you when I am weak
You taught me to be strong
And fight what's wrong
You are a boon to my curse
That made my life worse
Forever with me you will be
Because no one else has the key

41. Am I worthy?

Am I worthy of being your friend?
I am afraid our friendship will end
I know no longer where I stand
I hope you understand
We can't compare
That's why I am in despair
Just like you hope is rare
Your whispers I want to hear
Am I worthy?
That's what I doubt
My tears have turned into a drought
That's what I want to tell you about
The feeling I got for you
Through my words I let you know
Me and you friends forever
Our ship will sink never

42. My Little Town

Hurt and Pain
There's so much to gain
Peace and love
It's all the same
But how can I be so lost?
In a place I know so well
How am I so broken?
In a family so together
My little town was a perfect town
Where you would see no one frown
Except me
Feeling I've been sting by a bee
My town is a perfect town
Till you cross the tracks
There are rows and rows of memories
That are far away from my fantasies
My heart aching one
I've been shun
I weep, I cry
I plead, I try
Life is a lesson,
So learn it well.
Maybe one day
You can tell its tale

43. Hiding the Sadness, Hiding My Pain

Hiding the sadness, hiding my pain

All my efforts are going vain

Life isn't fair

That's why I cry in despair

My heart is aching

I burn from within

I feel like breaking

My happiness thrown in the bin

My skin is on fire

I want to fulfill my desire

The world must stay out

Without doubt

My calmness on my face is an ongoing sin

My smile is hardly a grin

I've been hiding behind a mask'

That's my task

44. Special People

You came as a ray of light,
Made my life cheerful and bright,
Showering your affection over me
So that my face was full of glee.
Taking away my complete loneliness
And giving me back all the happiness
With a Midas touch of your care
To keep me away from despair.
I'll never leave you midway,
And tales of our bond people will say

45. Hell In My Head

I found hell in my head
While laying on my bed
Uncertainty…uncertainty
Can it convert into certainty?
Perhaps
The saddest word
Sometimes thing seem blurred
My happiness is in a lapse
I feel like a wild beast
Trapped in an unblocked cage
The joy became creased
How can I take out my rage?
I feel like butterfly
Left all alone
On a hard,rock stone
No one will see me cry
Awfully afraid about what lies on the other side
What if they know I have cried?
I have something viciously brilliant inside
This thing is my pride

46. Jack

Once there was a young man named Jack
He lived in a village, out by the track
He worked hard each day, from dawn until dusk
But he never seemed to get ahead, no matter how hard he worked.
One day, Jack decided he'd had enough
He packed up his things and set off in a huff
He walked for days and nights on end
Until he reached a distant land.
This new place was a land of wonder
With mountains that reached up to the sky
Jack marveled at the beauty all around
And knew he had found a new home, at last.
He settled down in a cozy little house
And began working hard, just like a mouse
He planted seeds and tended to his garden
And soon he was living the life of a true bard.
Jack lived out his days in this new land
And though he missed his old home, he made the most of what he had
He was happy and content, living a simple life
And that's the story of Jack, the man with the heart of gold, and the
spirit of a true pioneer.

47. Magic

The forest was alive with the sound of music
As I wandered, lost and alone
I followed the sound of the flute's magic
Until I came upon a gnome
He sat on a mushroom, playing his instrument
His long beard flowed down to his toes
I stopped and listened, in awe and content
As the music washed over my soul
But as the song reached its final note
I blinked and the gnome was gone
In his place was a beautiful fairy, afloat
Her wings glowing in the dawn
I rubbed my eyes, sure I was dreaming
But no, she was there, fluttering near
She chuckled and said, "Surprised, are you seeming?
I'm more than just a gnome, my dear"
And with a wink and a wave, she flew away
Leaving me stunned and amazed
The twist in that tale, who could have foreseen?
A gnome who turns into a fairy, ablaze

48. My Future

I am a writer, reader, and lover of words
In the future, my pen will sing like birds
I'll write stories that touch the hearts of many
And I'll bring new worlds to life, oh so many
I'll delve into the depths of the human soul
And explore the mysteries that make us whole
I'll weave tales of love and loss, of joy and sorrow
And I'll take my readers on a journey, tomorrow
I'll immerse myself in the written word
And let my imagination be my guide, it's never deterred
I'll pour my heart and soul into every line
And with each new story, I'll truly shine
For the future is mine to create
And as a writer, I'll never be late
To capture the magic of the world around
And share it with all, with my pen unbound

49. Teachers

Teachers, oh how they shine
Guiding us through every subject and lesson of time
Their patience and kindness never seem to wane
As they strive to help us learn and maintain
They inspire us to reach for the stars
Encouraging us to set aside our doubts and scars
They are our rock, our foundation strong
Helping us to right our wrongs
They see the potential in each and every one of us
Helping us to discover and to trust
In ourselves and in our abilities to grow
And to tackle any challenge, high or low
Great teachers, you are the ones we turn to
When we need help, guidance, or simply a clue
You are the ones who lead us to success
And help us to overcome any stress
Your wisdom and experience are invaluable gifts
Helping us to navigate through life's twists and turns, shifts and shifts
Your dedication to your craft is truly admirable
And it is something that we will always be grateful
Great teachers, you are the ones who make a difference
In the lives of your students, without hesitation or indifference
You are the ones who inspire us to learn and to grow
And to become the best versions of ourselves that we can possibly be,
don't you know?

You are the mentors, the role models, the guides
Helping us to reach new heights and to take pride
In our achievements and in our progress
Thank you, great teachers, for all that you confess
Your tireless efforts and boundless energy
Inspire us to aim for the best and to be
The best that we can be, in every way
Thank you, great teachers, for leading the way.
Thank you, great teachers, for all that you do
For being an endless source of knowledge and virtue
You are the light that guides us on our way
And for that, we are forever grateful and will forever stay
Thank you for being the shining stars
That guide us through life's journey, near and far

For my readers

Thank you for reading till the end

Of the poems I have penned

It means the world to me

That you took the time to see

Into the words I wrote with care

And the emotions I did bare

Thank you for sticking with me

Until the very last line

It's readers like you

That make the writing worth it all the time

Turn over to dive into a beautiful world of zodiac

50. Aries

Aries, oh Aries,
A force to be reckoned with,
You blaze through life with fiery passion,
Leaving your mark wherever you go.
Your strength and determination,
Are an inspiration to all,
You never back down from a challenge,
But always stand tall.
Your courage knows no bounds,
You are always ready to take the lead,
Your zest for life is contagious,
Your spirit, oh so freed.
So here's to Aries,
A sign of the zodiac divine,
May your fire continue to burn bright,
And your bravery always shine.

51. Taurus

Taurus, oh Taurus,
A sign of strength and stability,
You stand firm, grounded and true,
With a resolve that is unshakeable.
Your determination is admirable,
You never give up or stray from your path,
You are dependable and reliable,
A rock for others to trust and clasp.
Your senses are keen,
And your appreciation for the finer things,
Is a joy for all to see,
You bring beauty and pleasure to everything.
So here's to Taurus,
A sign of dependability,
May your strength grow and resolve,
Inspire us all to be.

52. Gemini

Gemini, oh Gemini,
A sign of duality and wit,
Your mind is sharp and curious,
Your thoughts, quick and fit.
You are a social butterfly,
Flitting from group to group,
Your charisma and charm,
Leave a positive loop.
Your adaptability is enviable,
You can fit into any scene,
Your versatility is endless,
You are a master of the unseen.
So here's to Gemini,
A sign of intelligence and grace,
May your curious mind,
Forever seek and embrace.

53. Cancer

Cancer, oh Cancer,
A sign of intelligence and perfection,
Your conscientious nature,
Ensures that every task meets your high standards of selection.
You are a master of attention to detail,
Leaving nothing overlooked or undone,
Your drive for excellence,
Is second to none.
Your sharp mind is constantly seeking,
To learn and improve all that you do,
Your intelligence and diligence,
Are traits that set you apart and make you true.
So here's to Cancer,
A sign of intelligence and perfection,
May your drive to succeed,
Inspire all with its reflection.

54. Leo

Leo, oh Leo,
A sign of regality and pride,
You walk with your head held high,
Your confidence, unbridled and free.
Your passion and vitality,
Are contagious to all,
You are a force to be reckoned with,
And your spirit, will never fall.
Your creativity knows no bounds,
You are always seeking new ways to express,
Your generosity and kindness,
Are a blessing, not a stress.
So here's to Leo,
A sign of magnificence and light,
May your spirit continue to shine,
And your radiance, always ignite.

55. Virgo

Virgo, oh Virgo,
A sign of diligence and hard work,
You approach every task with care,
Leaving no room for shirk.
Your attention to detail is admirable,
You strive for perfection in all that you do,
Your analytical mind is sharp,
And your problem-solving skills, askew.
You are reliable and dependable,
A friend that one can trust,
Your hardworking nature,
Leaves no task left to rust.
You have a practical approach to life,
And a desire to always improve,
Your dedication to excellence,
Is a quality that we all can groove.
So here's to Virgo,
A sign of diligence and grace,
May your quest for perfection,
Forever guide your path and place.

56. Scorpio

Scorpio, oh Scorpio,
A sign of intensity and passion,
You approach life with fierce determination,
And your spirit, a flame that never abates.
Your intuition is strong,
And your perception, keen,
You are able to see through facades,
And into the hearts of those serene.
Your loyalty is unwavering,
And your love, fierce and true,
You are a force to be reckoned with, In all that you do.
So here's to Scorpio,
A sign of depth and emotion,
May your spirit continue to burn bright,
And your passions, be a beautiful ocean.

57. Saggitarius

Sagittarius, oh Sagittarius,
A sign of adventure and wanderlust,
Your spirit is free and wild,
And your thirst for knowledge, a must.
You are curious and open-minded,
Always seeking new experiences to try,
Your optimism and positivity, Are a beacon in the sky.
Your honesty is admirable, You speak the truth, no matter the cost,
Your wisdom and guidance, Are valued by all, no matter the cost.
So here's to Sagittarius, A sign of wanderlust and free spirit, May your
adventurous nature, Lead you on many a journey, meritorious.

58. Capricorn

Capricorn, oh Capricorn,
A sign of ambition and drive,
You strive for success in all that you do,
And your determination, will never wive.
Your practical nature is admirable,
You plan and execute with precision,
Your discipline and self-control,
Are a source of inspiration and vision.
Your loyalty and hard work,
Are unrivaled by any other,
You are a dependable friend,
And a valuable asset to discover.
So here's to Capricorn,
A sign of ambition and poise,
May your drive and determination,
Forever bring you joy and noise.

59. Aquarius

Aquarius, oh Aquarius,
A sign of innovation and progress,
You are always seeking new ways,
To improve and finesse.
Your open-mindedness is admirable,
You embrace change and the unknown,
Your creativity knows no bounds,
And your ideas, always shown.
You are a true humanitarian,
With a heart for helping others,
Your generosity and kindness,
Are a blessing to all your bothers.
So here's to Aquarius,
A sign of progress and reform,
May your innovative spirit,
Forever keep you warm.

60. Pisces

Pisces, oh Pisces,
A sign of sensitivity and emotion,
You are in tune with your feelings,
And your empathy, a beautiful potion.
Your creativity is boundless,
And your artistic talents, a true treasure,
You have a way of expressing yourself,
That brings beauty and pleasure.
Your intuition is strong,
And your perception, keen,
You are able to understand,
The thoughts and feelings of those unseen.
So here's to Pisces,
A sign of sensitivity and art,
May your creative spirit,
Forever play a vital part.

Thank You!

With gratitude my heart is filled,

For all the love and support you've instilled.

Your kindness and generosity,

Have touched my soul and set me free."

"With every word I pen to paper,

I'm reminded of the love and grace you've given.

Your unwavering support and encouragement,

Has been the light that guides me through the darkness.

From the bottom of my heart,

I thank you, For every smile you've brought and every tear you've dried.

For every laugh and every moment shared, I'll be forever grateful and never tired.

With every chapter I write,

I'll remember the role you've played in my life.

For you have helped me to be the best version of me,

And for that, I'll always be grateful, eternally.

So, thank you, dear friend, for being a part of my journey,

For being a light in the darkness and a love that's eternal.

You'll forever hold a special place in my heart, And in my words, you'll always be immortal."